GARDEN SEATS and BENCHES

ISBN 2-909838-43-9

Mattei Popovici

GARDEN SEATS and BENCHES

Introduction by Louis Benech

ALAIN de GOURCUFF ÉDITEUR

Far more than something to sit on

Gardens are places for looking, for contemplation, for reading, for reflection, for dreaming, for chatting, for philosophizing, for embracing — but could we do any of these things satisfactorily without that indispensable item of garden furniture, the bench or seat? Irresistible for moments of repose or poetic rêverie, they are as useful as they are delightful, making convenient and comfortable spots for keeping an eye on children at play, for sharing an al fresco lunch under a shady tree, or for quietly resting.

From the point of view of garden design, a bench or seat is far more than merely something to sit on, moreover. It may also serve as an eye-catcher to close a perspective, or as a lure for visitors strolling idly down paths and borders. Here, the ornamental qualities of garden seats come to the fore. They may boast charming curves, eccentric motifs or startling colours, or, as at the Villa Orsini (p.31), make thrilling reference to grotesque monsters. They may be scaled up, assuming larger proportions in order to appear temptingly closer, easier to reach. Or they may be shrunk to create a tantalizing sense of distance and exaggerated perspective. They may imitate the antique, complete with stone chimera, the Gothic or the Chinese style (p.71); they may be boldly geometric in wrought iron (p.75) or flowingly naturalistic — with motifs inspired by ferns, vine tendrils or lily-of-the-valley — in cast iron (p.81). And in the twenty-first century they are now available from supermarkets in a range of styles and synthetic materials.

———————

In addition to their ornamental role, seats and benches also fulfil a another function, more indirect and derived from the way they are placed within the garden. For once visitors have reached their goal, in the form of the seat at the end of the perspective, they invariably turn round — whereupon there unfolds a view in reverse of the perspective down which they have just strolled. The same trees, shrubs and flowers, lawns and paths, now create new vistas, reminding us that in a garden every view may be read in at least two different directions. Whatever the scale of a garden, whether broad and open or small and intimate, the play of light also plays a role of fundamental importance in the perception of colours and textures: viewed 'back to front', a shady vista may become flooded with light, or an open, luminous prospect may take on a more veiled, enigmatic quality. Receding planes suddenly shift to assume a different order, and it is to the ever-inviting bench or seat that we owe this richer view.

The positioning of seats may be subtler still, accompanying visitors' steps rather than making a goal for them, and providing skilfully placed pauses. By placing them at strategic points in his or her composition, the garden designer invites visitors to stop, linger and look, perhaps directing their gaze towards a precise point — and so transforming the seat into a viewpoint or belvedere.

At Méréville, for example, the tunnel leading to the Temple of Filial Piety was pierced with openings looking out over the gardens. Some of these were marked by benches, roughly cut into the rock and barely visible at first glance. They served as a subtle indication to visitors to pause at these precise spots in order to enjoy the best views of the picturesque features that dotted the gardens (of which a replica of Trajan's Column is the only surviving example). A similar ploy was used later at Les Buttes-Chaumont (1867), where the visitor's gaze was directed towards the windmills of Montmartre, on the site where the basilica of Sacré-Cœur now stands.

In their role as viewpoints, garden seats became necessarily static, thus coming full circle to rejoin the earliest examples of such features. These were described in the thirteenth century by Albertus Magnus, mentor of St Thomas Aquinas, in his encyclopaedic work *De Vegetalibus:* 'Between the flower beds and the grass, there shall be, at the very edge, square in shape and raised up, another stretch of pleasant flower-strewn turf, arranged as a sort of bench to serve as a restorative to the senses.'

As may be seen in medieval paintings and tapestries, turfed benches such as these were to become increasingly sophisticated, developing into seats topped with sweet-smelling thyme or camomile and contained at the sides by low walls of brick or stone. This immovable characteristic continued into the Renaissance, when benches were set on weighty marble legs in antique style, as at the Villa Borghese.

Only in the seventeenth century did the idea of moveable garden seats develop. In the early years of his reign, indeed, Louis XIV was in the habit of having armchairs brought out of his royal residences and placed

————————

about the gardens at his whim, to be taken inside again when they were no longer desired.

Henceforth, benches were to become fully-fledged 'garden furniture'; and like internal furniture, they were made of wood. Views of the gardens at Marly commissioned by Louis XIV from 1700 show quantities of such seats with balustraded backs, on which favoured courtiers were permitted to relax after a stroll through the 'green rooms' of the gardens. In his *Theory and Practice of Gardening, with a Full Discussion of some Handsome Gardens* (1739), Dezallier d'Argenville advised that they should be painted in order to preserve the wood: 'They should be painted with oil paint, in green or another colour, not only in order to preserve them but also for the sake of cleanliness.'

Forms remained within a limited range, however, although the occasional stroke of imagination would produce astonishing hybrid creations, such as fountain-seats (p.63).

Not until the nineteenth century, when visiting gardens became the popular pastime that it remains to this day, did garden seats and benches really come into their own. The development of new materials — and notably of cast iron — enabled new shapes and forms to flourish. Paradoxically, indeed, in an era when padded, upholstered comfort was becoming the rule for interior seat furniture, in garden seats considerations of comfort were almost invariably sacrificed to aesthetic and structural requirements. Less anthropomorphic than ever, garden seats now took

———————

their inspiration from a widely eclectic range of sources, both historical (p.69) and natural (p.61).

More recently, the quest for comfort — no longer subordinated to the need to use durable, rigid materials — has returned to the fore: seats have become lower, backs more curved and armrests more yielding. Exotic — and rot-resistant — woods, meanwhile, provide a contemporary take on the eternal, permanent qualities formerly supplied by cast iron. And imaginative variations on the theme continue to flourish in manifestations such as a bridge-seat (p.23), a neat combination of belvedere and tête-à-tête, or Renzo Piano's bench-seats.

The concept of designing garden seats in combination with their surroundings has become increasingly rare, except as part of an architectural ensemble such as Gaudì's Parque Güell in Barcelona (p.45). Benches are now moveable features, subject to the vicissitudes of changes in gardens and in the tastes of succeeding generations.

But wherever they may be and whatever form they may take — Gothic Revival, Japanese, Arts & Crafts or Cubist (as in the example carved by Laurens and now in the Ermitage Pompadour at Fontainebleau) — they remain devoted above all to those activities to which gardens are so pre-eminently suited: looking, contemplating, reading, thinking, dreaming...

[…] On a bench at the corner of some allée
We'll tell each other, sparing words,
The secrets that the little birds
Share beneath the branches' sway.

Alfred de Musset, *'Simone', Poésies nouvelles*

Marble seat

Schloss Sans-Souci, Potsdam

Nineteenth century

Stone 'fan' bench
Twentieth century

Bench of Japanese inspiration
Kiftsgate Court, Chipping Campden
Gloucestershire
Twentieth century

Cast-iron 'Oak & Ivy' bench
Coalbrookdale Company
Late nineteenth century

Bridge-seat

Rivière de la Calonne, Eure

Twentieth century

Cast-iron bench
Designed by Karl Friedrich Schinkel
Schloss Glienicke, Potsdam
*c.*1825

Cast-iron and marble bench
Designed by Karl Friedrich Schinkel
Berlin
*c.*1825

Wrought-iron bench
Barnard, Bishop and Barnard Ltd.
1930

'Grotesque' seat
Designed by Pyrrho Ligorio
Villa Orsini, Bomarzo, Italy
Sixteenth century

Bench in cast iron and wood
Designed by Karl Friedrich Schinkel
Märkisches Museum, Berlin
1828

'Stibadium'
Designed by Karl Friedrich Schinkel
Park Klein-Glienicke, Potsdam
1847

Cedar bench
Le Bois des Moutiers
Varengeville-sur-Mer, Seine-Maritime

'Semicircular' seat
Ireland
Early twentieth century

'Parasol' seats
From *Designs for Rural Residences*
Published by R. Ackermann
London, 1818

Cast-iron bench with
Gothic Revival motifs
The Metropolitan Museum of Art
New York
1850-60

Mosaic seat
Designed by Antonio Gaudí
Parque Güell, Barcelona
1900-14

Teak bench
After a design by Sir Edwin Lutyens
Early twentieth century

'Accolade' bench
Private collection
Early nineteenth century

Stone bench in Gothic Revival style
After Karl Friedrich Schinkel
Schloss Babelsberg, Potsdam
*c.*1840

Rustic wooden bench
United States
Early twentieth century

'Fern & Blackberry' bench
in cast iron and wood
Château Impney Hotel, Droitwich
1875

Wrought-iron games chair
and footrest on wheels
Private collection
1875

Circular tree seat

From *Ideenmagazin*

Published by I.G. Gromann

Leipzig, 1799

'Rustic Settee' in cast iron
The Metropolitan Museum of Art
New York
Second half of the nineteenth century

Fountain-seat
From *Ideenmagazin*
Published by I.G. Gromann
Leipzig, 1799

Bench in painted wood
Château de Chenonceaux
Nineteenth century

Stone bench
Ferdinando Gravina
Villa Palagonia, Sicily
Eighteenth century

'Medallion' bench
Coalbrookdale Company
1865

Wooden bench in Gothic Revival style
Designed by David Hicks
Great-Britain
Twentieth century

'Vine Pattern Garden Seat'
E.T. Barnum, Detroit
Henry Ford Museum & Greenfield Village
Dearborn
1845-50

'Osmunda Regalis' bench
with bracket shelves, in cast iron
Coalbrookdale Company
Ironbridge George Museum Trust

'Swan' bench
France
1950

'Pollards' bench
La Valeterie, Calvados
Twentieth century

Cast-iron bench
Upper garden, Palace of Tsarsköe Selo
Russia
Nineteenth century

'Wheelbarrow' bench
Designed by Sir Edwin Lutyens
Chatsworth, Derbyshire
Early twentieth century

Stone bench
Palace of Versailles
Twentieth century

Bench in wrought iron and wood
Germany
1797

Bench in painted wood
with baluster back
Denmark
Nineteenth century

Cast-iron bench
Designed by Claude Lalanne
France
Twentieth century

Printed in 2000
for ALAIN de GOURCUFF ÉDITEUR

Designed by Maxence Scherf

Phototypeset, photogravure and printing by
Imprimerie Escourbiac, Graulhet (Tarn), France